HELPING STUDENTS OVERCOME ROADBLOCKS TO ACHIEVEMENT

by Regenia Mitchum Rawlinson, M.Ed., NCSC, NCC

Strategies and Activities to Help Students Triumph Over Problems with Motivation, Anger and Disconnection

GRADES 5-12

youth light
inc.

© 2005 by YouthLight, Inc.
Chapin, SC 29036

Design and Layout by Diane Florence • Project Editing by Susan Bowman

ISBN
1889636819

Library of Congress Number
2004116311

10 9 8 7 6 5 4 3 2 1
Printed in the United States

⟩ DEDICATION

To my husband David, who is my best friend and strongest advocate, and my children David, Bradford, and Brittany who taught me more about myself than I thought I needed to learn. My husband and my children also taught me how to recognize the important things in life. They are my inspiration and my joy. I am very proud of them.

To all of the fine teachers and administrators who work with students each day. They build tomorrow's leaders. Hope this book will help them in this effort.

To my mother who birthed seventeen children and knows the value of the human spirit and how to uplift it and encourage it.

⟩ ABOUT THE AUTHOR

Regenia Mitchum Rawlinson, M.Ed., NCC, NCSC has been an educator for over 28 years. She has served as a Special Education Teacher, elementary counselor, and high school guidance counselor and director.

Since 1997 Mrs. Rawlinson, co-founder of Village Concepts, has been sharing her ideas and insights about motivation - and how to help educators and other professionals assist discouraged and angry students to excel. She has conducted numerous workshops and seminars on the local, state, and national levels. She received her B.A. from Winthrop College. She earned her master's degree from Winthrop University. She lives in South Carolina with her husband, David; they have three children ranging in age from 17-28.

TABLE OF CONTENTS

THE CHALLENGE

Toxically motivated, angry, and disconnected students - sound familiar? When the bell rings for the first time to signal the beginning of the new school year, hundreds of these students march in. They enter with all the other smiling faces without a hint of what is really behind their cheery appearance.

But once in the classroom, they sometimes can exhibit toxic motivation, anger, and show signs of being disconnected from the learning process. William Glasser, author of *Counseling with Choice Theory: The new Reality Therapy* (2001) believes that students have a reason for behaving in a particular manner. Glasser believes that children misbehave to avoid a less appealing or less painful alternative.

When teachers plan their academic instruction for a class, they expect participation and contribution from all students. However, toxically motivated, angry, and disconnected students show little interest in classroom activities and refuse to participate. Teachers are frustrated with the attitude and behavior of some students. As a result, teacher/student relationships sometimes become strained and ultimately result in a vicious power struggle. This power struggle may eventually escalate leading to a referral to an administrator, sometimes for the smallest infraction. Consequently, an environment of hostility can be created in the classroom and opportunities for learning are lessened significantly.

The task of managing student behavior in a hostile classroom environment and maintaining an environment that is conducive to learning for all students can become overwhelming and complex. Managing student behavior in the classroom presents a greater challenge when students are toxically motivated, angry, and have disconnected from the learning process. The success of the teacher to manage the behavior of these students will depend upon the techniques and strategies the teacher selects to encourage disconnected students to engage in the learning process (Coil, 2001).

Teachers need to have a thorough understanding of what causes toxically motivated, angry and disconnected students to exhibit disruptive behavior. This understanding will enable teachers to determine the most appropriate techniques and strategies to use with these students to engage them in the learning process. Professional educators and community members oftentimes offer a variety of explanations. Most will agree that home environment, significant others, caretakers, societal influences, experiences, personalities, and other factors each play a part in determining the moods and goals the students bring to the classroom.

I have concluded after working with students for close to three decades that a reason students bring toxic motivation, anger, and disconnectedness to the classroom is because these students feel limited in their ability to participate in the classroom environment in meaningful and expected ways. They have met with repeated failure in the past and they fear more of the same. This leaves them feeling powerless with a deepening need for positive affirmations. William Glasser, author and behavioral expert believes that all human beings have five basic needs: love, freedom, power, fun, and belonging. Glasser also believes that a person will do whatever it takes for as long as it takes to meet a perceived need to the point of one's personal satisfaction. Unfortunately, for some students, this process could take years and an enormous about of emotional and psychological energy. This happens partly because these students lack a clear understanding of how to satisfy their need resulting in motivation, anger, and disconnectedness.

When students believe that they are failures and think they will continue to fail in the future, poor decision-making can be perpetuated. Poor decisions can have a direct impact on academic achievement. Some educators refer to this as the failure syndrome and some define it as learned helplessness (Brophy, 1998, Lumsden, 1994).

These students eventually feel unworthy, unloved, and powerless to change their circumstances. They also view their environment as hostile, uncaring, and unresponsive to their needs. Once these unhealthy views become fully integrated into their psyches, their behaviors mirror their views and manifest in a variety of negative ways. Regrettably, the negative ways in which students manifest their behaviors are through aggression and frustration. Mary Fitzsimmons (1998) suggests that a nurturing and caring environment is one means of providing an antidote for aggression and frustration.

I have worked with thousands of students over the years. Some were motivated to achieve in school while others were like the students I have described here. The most common characteristics among students who wanted to achieve were:

- they felt empowered to offer something to others
- they felt accepted by others
- they felt valued by others
- they felt respected by others
- they exhibited high self-esteem and self-worth

Educators are presented with a great challenge to create environments and opportunities that can enhance learning and encourage motivation, angry, and disconnected students to fully engage in the learning process. Jeremy Brophy (1998) suggests that this environment can be created when teachers provide support, encouragement, and task assistance. Stephen Covey (1990) agrees and emphasizes the importance of teachers communicating care and respect for students to aid in the creation of encouraging classroom environments.

Most students will thrive in a caring classroom environment and for toxically motivated, angry, and disconnected students such an environment has enormous benefits. Overwhelmingly, research has shown schools that make it a priority of meeting students' basic human needs of support, caring, empathy, acceptance, and respect, foster motivation to learn (Purkey, 1999, Bonnie, Lumsden,1997). The indication is clear, if professional educators want to provide the best possible learning environment for students, they must send a clear message that they care not only about what students learn but also how students learn and what they need.

ENHANCING ACADEMIC ACHIEVEMENT

> *"I am only one, but still I am one. I cannot do everything, but still I can do something; And because I cannot do everything, I will not refuse to do the something I can do."*
>
> EDWARD EVERETT HALE

Understanding how the behaviors of one person can be influenced by the behaviors of another person is necessary when attempting to answer the question of how to improve academic achievement. Since research has shown that academic achievement is directly linked to high self-esteem (Reasoner, 2004), it is important that students develop and maintain a sense of significance, competence, and acceptance to foster academic achievement. Achievement can cause a big boost to self-esteem. Professional educators agree that when students are achieving, they make healthier life choices and manage themselves in acceptable and productive ways.

Students achieve at a higher level when they feel affirmed by others in their environment. Some educators have suggested a variety of reasons why students do not feel affirmed. However, my experience as a counselor and teacher, coupled with my interaction with other professionals, has led me to believe that there are two basic reasons for not feeling affirmed, fractured families and unaffirming environments. Fractured families are families without the emotional capacity necessary to foster high self-esteem; with regular occurrence of violence and abuse, authoritarian parenting style, no established behavioral standards, and drug use and abuse is considered fractured families (Weiss and Schwarz, 1996). These family conditions and environments leave some children feeling devalued resulting in low self-esteem which often can negatively impact academic achievement. The need to feel valued is so important to these children that academic achievement becomes less important.

Some professional educators suggest that schools should and must share the burden of providing support and services to parents to improve academic achievement. By providing parental support that encourages parents to modify and adjust their behavior may help ensure their child's success. Some teachers and administrators, object to making schools responsible for resolving the family problems that have lead to school failure. The teachers and administrators raising these objections are correct and justified in their assessment of their role. They cannot force parents to change. The mere suggestion of change to some parents can bring about anger and make some parents hostile toward the school. However, professional educators can help students organize and restructure their thoughts about their home environment in a way that reduces toxic motivation, discouragement, anger, and disconnection.

Educators can also create warm and nurturing classrooms and schools that would offset some of the negative impact of the home environment. Many educators argue that providing students with nurturing classrooms and school environments will not lessen the

ENHANCING ACADEMIC ACHIEVEMENT *(continued)*

effects of the home environments that are lacking in the level of support needed to encourage academic achievement.

Some educators also believe that until the home environment changes, the student's behavior will not change. Educators who work under this assumption do a grave injustice to their students. Bonnie Benard (1997) in her article, "Turning it Around for All Youth: From Risk to Resilience" suggests that it only takes one caring adult to positively impact the behavior and performance of students. Good, Grumley, & Roy (2003, p.7) authors of, *A Connected School*, suggest that if children do not receive nurturing at home, they have little chance of having this basic need met if it is not met at school

Most educators spend more than forty hours each week with some students. Phillip Schlechty (2001, p.69) in his book, *Shaking Up The School House*, suggests that the behavior of educators has a direct impact on how and what students are motivated to achieve and on how they behave. The following are ten strategies that encourage greater student achievement and improved student behavior.

1. BE A GOOD LISTENER

(Covey, 1990). Accomplished educators understand where the students are coming from and see this understanding as a necessary factor to effectively interact with students. Students need to be understood, affirmed, validated, and appreciated on a regular basis.

2. COMMUNICATE EFFECTIVELY

(Irmsher, 1996). An essential component of effective communication is knowledge of the student's cultural background and how that culture influences thoughts and behaviors. Communication is likely to occur between individuals when they understand the language of each other. In addition, outside communication is important so the school and community are aware of what is going on in the classroom. This can help you gain support and let others know what your students are doing (Sutton, 1999).

3. BE CAREFUL OF YOUR PERCEPTION.

Linda Lumsden (1994) in her research found that there is a direct correlation between teacher perception and student achievement. Her research clearly points out, consciously or unconsciously, that some teachers tend to behave differently toward children who are from families not adversely affected by one or more of the following five social factors that put children at risk than they do toward children whom these factors have negatively affected.

- poverty
- family composition
- mother's education
- race and ethnicity
- language background

Other researchers (Tauber, 1998, Brophy, 1998, Benard, 1997, Omatoni and Omatoni, 1996, Bamburg, 1994, Cotton 1989) agree and specify how teacher perception can manifest in the classroom based on how they perceive individual or groups of students.

ENHANCING ACADEMIC ACHIEVEMENT *(continued)*

When student(s) are perceived by teachers to have high ability based on one of the five factors some teachers tend to use more inviting body language and tone of voice. The opposite is true when students are perceived by teachers to have low ability based on those same factors.

4. VIEW INTELLIGENCE AS DYNAMIC AND FLUID

(Lumsden, 1997). If teachers believe instruction and effective teaching strategies have little or no effect on a student's ability to learn, their efforts to help students will be compromised and limited.

5. VARY YOUR INSTRUCTIONAL PRACTICES

(Schwartza, 2001). Varied instruction accommodates all learning styles. Effective curricula and instructional strategies engage students' interest, promote inquiry and discovery, and provide students with a sense of satisfaction from their own efforts. You have heard the term, "Variety is the spice of life." Variety also spices up student learning.

6. BE SENSITIVE TO CULTURAL DIVERSITY

(Payne, 2003, Schwartza, 2001). Include activities that involve all cultures represented in the classroom. Accept all students and focus on the positive strengths of each one.

7. MAINTAIN A SAFE AND ORDERLY ENVIRONMENT

(Schwartza, 2001). Maintain a safe and orderly environment where educators and students demonstrate a respect for each other.

8. BE SENSITIVE TO THE FEELINGS OF STUDENTS.

How students feel about school, classroom, and teachers impact how much they are willing to participate. Effective teachers listen to the needs of the students and show empathy and compassion (Kratzer, 1996).

9. DEVELOP A POSITIVE RELATIONSHIP WITH EACH STUDENT IN THE CLASS.

Take time to learn about their dreams, goals, likes, and dislikes. Learn as much about them as possible. Make this priority #1 and it will pay big dividends. Students will feel cared about and they will want to take part in the learning process. Students learn from those they like and respect and who like and respect them (McFadden and Cooper, 2004).

10. PRACTICE SELF-EVALUATION.

"Learning about one's personal strengths is an important step toward building the kind of self-confidence and positive motivation that can last a lifetime," (Anonymous). Accomplished educators know the benefits of a comprehensive periodic self-evaluation.

ENHANCING ACADEMIC ACHIEVEMENT *(continued)*

Self-evaluation is valuable in critiquing behavior to ascertain the impact of those behaviors. Self-evaluation supports the desire of educators who want to enhance student motivation in the classroom. The evaluative process is comprehensive when the educators examine:

- their belief system about students
- why they do what they do
- why they interact with students the way they do
- how they interact with students
- views about "high-risk" students
- views and beliefs about culture
- what they believe about teaching
- the curriculum (relevant, culturally sensitive, contextual, challenging, achievable goals)

When educators evaluate their own behavior, they are taking a crucial step towards discovering what motivates students to achieve academically in the classroom. Additionally, the next step is also important for professional educators to take if they want students to establish a pattern of achievement. Educators must be willing to change their attitudes and behavior if they find it is contributing to students' apathy and disconnectedness from the learning process. Changing attitudes and behaviors will not be easy for professional educators to accomplish. Nevertheless, it is necessary if professional educators want to achieve the ultimate goal of helping students overcome roadblocks to achievement.

9

HOW TO USE THIS BOOK

Toxic motivation, anger, and disconnection are all roadblocks to achievement. The lessons in this book will offer suggestions, activities, and strategies to help professional educators address these three roadblocks to achievement. Academic achievement directly correlates to these and the need to systematically address them is necessary to increase the probability of students improving standardized test scores and reducing discipline referrals. If these roadblocks are not eliminated, students who fall prey to them may be left behind.

The reason for developing these lessons was my desire to offer materials to teachers and counselors that would encourage academic achievement. From my experience working with these students, I knew the lessons needed to be authentic and provide opportunities for students to practice. The lessons also needed to be adaptable to the needs and levels of the students and foster a sense of empowerment to help them make decisions to achieve in the classroom.

It is my hope that the lessons in this book are used liberally to address the needs of all students. Therefore, the professional educator who is using these lessons should seek to make adjustments when and where necessary. These activities and lessons are not intended to be comprehensive in addressing the problem of poor academic performance, but rather serve as a catalyst for further work in this area by the professional educator.

To help facilitate the success of each lesson, begin and end each lesson in this book with the following strategies:

- Shake students' hands or give a "high five" as they enter and exit the room.

- Allow students, before beginning the lesson, an opportunity to share concerns about things that have happened to them during the day/week.

- Allow students to evaluate each lesson. Use the evaluation form found in the appendix.

- End on a high by having students read the following affirmations (see next page).

AFFIRMATIONS

I am THE FUTURE.

I am A DREAMER.

I am A CREATOR.

I am THE PROMISE OF TOMORROW.

I am WISE.

I am A GOOD DECISION MAKER.

I am A RESPONSIBLE PERSON

I am FILLED WITH TALENTS AND GIFTS.

I am SUCCESSFUL.

I am A GOOD STUDENT.

I am A GOOD PERSON.

I am LOVABLE.

I am A KIND PERSON.

I am THE BEST ME THAT I CAN BE.

I am SMART IN MANY AREAS.

I am MY MOTHER'S CHILD

I am MY DADDY'S CHILD.

I am A THINKER.

I am A BELIEVER and BELIEVE IN MANY THINGS.

I am A PLANNER.

ROADBLOCK 1

Toxic Motivation

"We trifle when we assign limits to our desires, since nature hath set none."

— WILLIAM MAKEPEACE THACKERAY

INTRODUCTION

Toxic motivation is used here to mean how students are motivated to behave in ways that could negatively impact academic achievement. Toxic motivation often shows up in failure to complete class assignments and homework, class disruptions, suspensions, expulsions, poor grades, truancy, and disengagement from the learning process. Participation in the learning process is what educators desire from all students. However, some educators often find themselves trying to understand why some students fully engage in the learning process while others disengage. Understanding why this happens has been a challenge faced by some educators since record keeping on student achievement was originated.

Some professional educators are asking questions to help them understand why some students choose to disengage from the learning process by exhibiting toxic motivation. Many of these questions are:
• What can I do to help motivate students to engage in the learning process?

• What do I believe about students?

• How are children motivated to engage in the learning process?

Inherent in these questions are the following assumptions:
• Students can be motivated to engage in the learning process.

• It is the job of the educator to motivate students.

• Knowing the reasons will help educators motivate students to engage in the learning process

These assumptions suggest professional educators are responsible for motivating students to engage in the learning process. The assumptions have spawned new account-ability laws that require educators to improve test scores or explain the reasons for not meeting standards.

Since the response to these questions have produced limited success in providing educators with effective tools for motivating some students to engage in the learning process another approach is warranted. What if educators changed these questions to:
• Who is motivated to engage in the learning process?

• Does motivation always lead to high academic achievement?

• Is motivation a product or a process?

• What does the student believe?

• How can educators motivate students to engage in the process?

Included in this section are suggestions and activities for how to increase student's motivation to achieve.

WHO IS MOTIVATED?
Most three, four, and five year old children enter school excited. Some of these children maintain their excitement with each succeeding year. But, many gradually become apathetic and passive about participating in the educational process. In fact, one out of every four students will leave school before graduating (Lumsden, 1994). By the fourth grade, some of these students avoid participating in school activities, grades decline, and referrals for discipline begin to mount.
What happens to cause some students to exhibit toxic motivation? What motivates some students to engage in the learning process? Professional educators need answers to these questions if they are to help students become high achievers. One answer could be that students reap benefits from engaging in

the learning process or exhibiting toxic motivation. Some students believe that they reap benefits based on what they believe and how they exhibit their beliefs. If they believe that earning good grades is a benefit of engaging in the learning process, they will likely do what is required to earn good grades. Conversely, if they believe suspension is a benefit of exhibiting toxic motivation, they will likely behave in a manner that will result in suspension.

DOES MOTIVATION ALWAYS LEAD TO HIGH ACHIEVEMENT?

Motivation does not automatically translate into high academic achievement. If you accept the premise that all students are motivated, then you simultaneously acknowledge that motivation can lead to academic success or failure. Some students who succeed are motivated to succeed. Some students who fail are motivated to fail. The reason for their success or failure varies with the student's goals and beliefs about him/herself, the environment (school, home, community), and outlook. If the student's outlook on the future is positive and self-esteem is high, the student will strive for academic success. On the other hand, if the student has a negative outlook and poor self-esteem, the student will choose the path of apathy and, therefore, failure. The school environment can also contribute to a student's success or failure. Students are more likely to succeed in a school environment with caring educators who provide engaging work, safe surroundings, and opportunities to achieve.

WHAT DOES THE STUDENT BELIEVE?

This question is at the heart of why students engage in the learning process or exhibit toxic motivation. Some students live their lives based on how they see themselves, how they believe others view them, and what they believe about their abilities to achieve academically in school. Some students come to believe that they are incapable of achieving in the school or classroom environment. Professional educators could possibly eliminate these beliefs and thereby lessen the negative impact of toxic motivation by creating caring environments that provide successful opportunities. The more some of these students experience success, the more confidence they will gain in their capacity to achieve.

Larry Lashway (2003) found in his research that providing a caring environment is a primary factor in student achievement. Professional educators can create a caring environment verbally and nonverbally by:

- Establishing a positive relationship with students

- Encouraging students to use their personal strengths

- Acknowledging students' uniqueness, diversity, ideas, and beliefs

- Making an effort to include students in every aspect of the learning process

- Soliciting and accepting contributions from students to the learning process

- Modeling appropriate behaviors and attitudes

- Demonstrating consistency in the learning environment

- Avoiding having to remind students of past mistakes and allowing those mistakes to cloud judgment and hinder them from being open to student growth

- Exhibiting high expectations for student learning and behavior

- Modeling respect

- Disciplining (love, nurture, forewarn, correct) with the intent of changing behavior not punishing students

IS MOTIVATION A PRODUCT OR PROCESS?

For some students, a belief that failure is imminent is formulated gradually over time and due to a number of negative experiences. When some students meet with repeated failure, motivation to engage in the learning process is diminished (Tamber, 1998). These students believe they cannot succeed and they stop trying.

When students internalize these beliefs, they help shape student behavior. Internalization of beliefs is the second step in determining the nature of the motivation. These behaviors can be constructive or destructive. Constructive behaviors are likely to perpetuate success. Conversely, destructive behaviors will likely perpetuate a cycle of failure.

Patterns of behaviors are generally exhibited in every area of the student's life including the learning environment. Some teachers are frustrated by the exhibition of toxic motivation by some students and some students are equally annoyed by the teacher's insistence that they shape up. The result is an impasse that teachers and students find difficult to overcome.

Motivation is definitely a process that includes the stages discussed previously:
- interaction with others and environment
- internalization of beliefs
- formulation of personal beliefs
- exhibition of beliefs

Motivation is a process that begins with interaction. Accomplished educators, recognize the benefits of interacting positively with students. They realize interacting positively with students will impact how students will exhibit motivation in the classroom. An intense focus on each stage of motivation is necessary to facilitate a change in how students exhibit motivation. It is unlikely that a focus on only one stage will bring about full engagement in the learning process.

HOW CAN EDUCATORS MOTIVATE STUDENTS?

The role of educators in motivating students to achieve academically is a very important one and cannot be overstated. Over the years, some educators have asked, "What can I do to motivate students to engage in the learning process?" Some educators look for the answer in doing more, when the answer is likely to be found in doing less or doing what they already do differently. Providing a nurturing, safe, and caring environment for students is one of the most important steps professional educators can take to motivate students.

The activities in this section are designed to stimulate discussion. Therefore, students may introduce various issues that cannot possibly be included in this material. Professional educators are encouraged to draw from their own experiences and knowledge without imposing their views on the students. If information is not readily available on issues the students introduced, professional educators are encouraged to research and inform students of the findings at the next scheduled meeting.

Each activity in this section can be used independently. Each lesson will provide an opportunity for students to get acquainted and/or learn more about each other. In addition, students will learn to develop skills helpful in eliminating toxic motivation, which is a roadblock to achievement. You are also invited to select lessons most appropriate for your group. Good Luck and I wish you the best!

GET ACQUAINTED

OBJECTIVE(S):
- To provide opportunities for students to get acquainted
- To give an overview of the Lessons

PROCEDURE(S):
Have students sit in a circle. Hand one person a bag of skittles and ask him/her to take five skittles as he/she passes the bag to the next person. Continue until all students have taken some skittles. Ask each person to take turns telling one positive thing about themselves for each color of skittles they have.

Next, discuss the purpose for the lessons and how often they will be presented. Explain that they will have an opportunity to learn ways in which they can enhance their lives and to learn techniques that can make their lives more productive.

Provide an overview of all lessons by displaying the title of each lesson with brief statements of the content.

SUMMARY:
Ask students to share their feelings and impressions about the lesson topics.

ACTIVITY 1.1

IT'S ALL RELEVANT!

OBJECTIVE(S):
- For students to examine the meaning and purpose of life
- To emphasize the concept that everyone is special and therefore has something unique to offer

PROCEDURE(S):
Write the following quote on the board or display in some manner. Discuss with students.
"The biggest obstacle to reaching ones full potential is not knowing one's purpose."

Display pictures of several animals and describe characteristics and behaviors of each. Ask the students to list the behaviors of each animal and their beliefs about why these animals behave in this manner on a flip chart or separate piece of paper. Ask them to list the special abilities these animals possess which enable them to behave in this fashion.

Ask students to list the behaviors of people (i.e. laugh, sing, talk, build, think) and the reason for their behavior. Ask them to list the abilities of people that enable them to behave in these manners.

Continue in the same manner with other examples until the students have a clear grasp of the principle everything has a purpose or reason for being.

Ask students to discuss the similarities between people and animals. How are they alike? How does human behavior differ from animal behavior? What is the purpose of these animals? What is the purpose of each human being?

Ask them to write down what they believe their own purpose is as a human being. Explain to the students they may not fully know what their purpose is as an individual, although they may have some idea. Explain to the students that understanding their purpose as a human being is a good place to start. Additionally, ask them to list all the things they possess which enable them to fulfill their purpose. Discuss.

Note: When students list attributes that they possess as a human being, if they do not include mind, power of choice, speech, feelings, gifts, talents, ability, etc., you need to list and emphasize them.

SUMMARY:
Summarize by emphasizing the following points:
- Every person has a purpose.
- Everything and everyone has attributes to fulfill that purpose - collectively and individually.

However, these attributes need to be used to develop skills. If you want to reach your full potential, knowing your purpose is essential.

WHAT MAKES ME TICK?

OBJECTIVE(S):
- To explore and examine the various personality types
- To identify their personality types

PROCEDURE(S):
Distribute and discuss worksheet: **Who Am I?** Discuss the various personality types and their identifying characteristics.

Have students complete a simple personality profile. Sample personality profiles can be found on the Internet by searching for words such as personality profile, personality tests, etc. It is recommended that you search the internet for these personality profiles and not the students.

Have students share their results in a small group.

SUMMARY:
Summarize by emphasizing the following points:
- Your personality, in large part, determines what you like, how you react to various people and circumstances, how you handle situations, and what career choices you make.

- Having a real sense of what makes you tick can help you reach your full potential.

WHO AM I?

Directions: Review each personality type and select the personality type that best fits you. Then think about family members living with you and select the personality type that best fit each family member. (Then complete page 20)

INDEPENDENT/ARTISTIC

- ❑ Risk taker
- ❑ Self-starter
- ❑ Free spirited
- ❑ Dynamic
- ❑ Impulsive
- ❑ Rebellious
- ❑ Own individual
- ❑ Adaptable

PROFESSIONAL/RATIONAL

- ❑ Decisive
- ❑ Focused
- ❑ Likes practical but elegant surroundings
- ❑ Protect those close to them
- ❑ Relies on reason
- ❑ Goal oriented
- ❑ Constantly seeking knowledge
- ❑ Strong-willed

ANALYTICAL/CONFIDENT

- ❑ Take charge personality
- ❑ Logical
- ❑ Practical problem-solver
- ❑ Sophisticated
- ❑ Concrete
- ❑ Hard worker
- ❑ Dependable
- ❑ Realistic

PEACEFUL/IDEALISTIC

- ❑ Sensitive
- ❑ Easy to get along with
- ❑ Authentic
- ❑ Romantic
- ❑ Seeks strong relationships
- ❑ Initiative
- ❑ Appreciative
- ❑ Time alone is important

Adapted from *The Temperament Sorter II* by David Keirsey (1998) and from *What Type Are You?* by Ulla Zang (1998-2004). Both personality tests can be viewed, in part or whole, on the Internet by typing in keywords David Keirsey, Ulla Zang, or personality tests.

WHAT IS YOUR TYPE?

Directions: Write the names of family members living in your home. Write the personality type that best describes each member and characteristics of this personality type.

Name of family member	Personality type that best describes this family member	Characteristics of personality type

ACTIVITY 1.3

FAMILY AFFAIR

OBJECTIVE(S):
• To examine how personality types of family members influence behavior and relationships within the family

PROCEDURE(S):
Distribute the worksheet: Who Am I? Review personality types and the characteristics of each type. Distribute worksheet: What is Your Type? Ask students to complete and discuss responses.

Discuss the differences and similarities. Ask them to identify the students who are most like them and least like them. Discuss the impact the different personalities have on relationships within the families.

Ask students to share something new they learned about each family member and how this new information can be used to help them build better relationships with each family member.

Note: Use same procedure to discuss teachers, peers, etc.

SUMMARY:
Summarize by emphasizing the following points:
• Each personality type has certain identifying characteristics.
• Personality influences how you view life, the world, mannerisms, and how you react to various situations, and how you view others.

ACTIVITY 1.4

BEST KEPT SECRET

OBJECTIVE(S):
• To examine heritage as it relates to human beings

PROCEDURE(S):
Display on a flipchart, board or overhead transparency the word heritage (birthright, endowment, entitlement, estate, inheritance, legacy).

Discuss the meaning (something received from a parent or predecessor). It implies anything passed on to heirs or succeeding generations but applies to possessions other than actual property or money (traits of character, tradition). For example, when an individual has a will, whatever is owned is passed along to the heirs. The heirs then have the privilege and the right to use whatever is passed along to them in any way they choose. In the same way, human traits were passed along to you and you have the right to use them in any manner chosen.

Ask the students to list those traits that are uniquely human (ability to think, free will, choice). List and Discuss.

Distribute the **Human Heritage Will.**

Ask the students to respond to the following questions:
• What are some ways humans can use their heritage to positively impact the lives of others?
• What are some ways humans can use their heritage to negatively affect the lives of others?
• List the responses and discuss.

Emphasize that when humans use their heritage to influence the lives of others positively, the entire human race benefits in many ways. If an individual uses human traits in a negative sense, the human race suffers demoralization. To illustrate this point, tell about two strikingly different personalities such as Dr. Martin Luther King and Adolf Hitler (these are only suggestions). Point out that they had the same human heritage but chose to manifest them differently. The facilitator is encouraged to choose personalities that would be most relevant to the audience.

SUMMARY:
Summarize by emphasizing the following points:
• Human heritage is a gift.
• Human heritage is a privilege.
• Human heritage can be used in any manner chosen by the individual.
• The manner in which human heritage is used determines how others are affected.
• The manner in which human heritage is used and handled effects the quality of life of the individual.

HUMAN HERITAGE WILL

"We, your ancestors, being of sound mind and body, do set forth our hand this day, the first day of human existence, to this document from now on to be known as the last will and testament for every human being. We hereby decree the following to each person belonging to the human race:

- Free will
- Compassion
- Gifts
- Kindness
- Power of choice
- Capacity to learn
- Truth
- Respect
- Individuality
- Ability to reason
- Love
- Feelings

- Talents
- Integrity
- Conscience
- Empathy
- Justice
- Distinct physical features
- Ability to invent
- The right to be totally and completely free of anything that would enslave and bind
- The right to achieve personal excellence

We hereby acknowledge that each person has the right to use them in his or her own way. Therefore, each must remember that all choices, good or bad, have accompanying and corresponding consequences. Knowing this let all beware of how the property set forth in this document is used. Furthermore, when they are used exclusively for self-fulfillment, they can and will be destructive to the individual and others.

Your signature below verifies that you know and acknowledge that you are a member of the human race, and so being, have the aforementioned."

Signature _____

I AM WHAT I AM!

OBJECTIVE(S):
• To examine roles of individuals and the impact those roles have on others

PROCEDURE(S):
Discuss with students that people play many different roles. Ask students to identify some roles people play and list them on the board. For example, roles may include mother, sister, aunt, co-worker, student, friend, etc. Ask students to name the responsibilities associated with each role.

Distribute worksheet: **I Am What I Am.** Ask students to complete.

Discuss. As a follow-up question, ask what would result if they fail to fulfill their role(s).

Ask students to list roles they would like to improve. For example, they may want to do a better job in their role as a sister or brother.

SUMMARY
Summarize by emphasizing the following points:
• Every individual has multiple roles they play.
• Each role has it own responsibilities.
• How well you fill each role can increase your self-esteem.
• The extent to which you fulfill your roles determines the impact you have on the lives of others.

I AM WHAT I AM!

Directions: Put a check by each that applies to you and list the responsibilities that accompany each role. You may also add other roles and responsibilities.

❏ Student Responsibilities

_____

❏ Brother Responsibilities

_____

❏ Grandson Responsibilities

_____

❏ Uncle Responsibilities

_____

❏ Friend Responsibilities

_____

❏ Sister Responsibilities

_____

❏ Helper Responsibilities

_____

❏ Daughter/Son Responsibilities

_____

❏ List other roles and responsibilities here. _____

_____

ACTIVITY 1.6

RESCUE ME

OBJECTIVE(S):
• To familiarize students with community resources and assistance available to address various needs

PROCEDURE(S):
Invite persons from a variety of community agencies to participate as a part of a panel. Ask panelists to bring information about their agencies to share with the students. Have students create a teen directory that includes names, phone numbers, and addresses. Make this directory available to all students. Check with your school's policy before inviting a representative from an agency or organization.

Suggested agencies to invite:

• Social Services
• Mental health
• Health Department
• Department of Youth Services
• Crisis Pregnancy
• Substance Abuse Agency
• Rape Crisis
• Legal Services
• Teen Council
• Police Department

SUMMARY:
Allow students to ask questions and allow panelists to emphasize important points to remember.

ACTIVITY 1.7

WHAT'S HAPPENING

OBJECTIVE(S):
• To familiarize students with community agencies that offer activities in which to be involved

PROCEDURE(S):
Invite community agencies, clubs, civic organizations and school officials to share the programs and activities available to students. Also ask community agencies to come prepared to discuss job openings and offer opportunities to interview for available jobs.

Suggested panelists:

• YMCA/YWCA
• Director or person in charge of clubs and activities for youth
• Parks and Recreation
• Representatives from community centers
• Police Department (Explores programs for youth)
• Boy Scouts/Girls Scouts of America
• Daycare Centers
• Nursing Homes
• Athletic Director from school
• Leader for peer support programs at school (peer helping, peer mediation, etc)
• City Year
• United Way
• Project Challenge and other outward bound programs
• 4-H Program Leader

Have students create a bulletin board of all the resources available for youth in the community. Display this somewhere near the main office.

SUMMARY:
Ask students to list all the activities that interest them. Then have students make a check next to the one or two they are going to participate in.

ROADBLOCK 2

Student Anger

"Anger is rarely expressed rationally or intellectually."

— DAVID L. RAWLINSON

INTRODUCTION

Anger is a powerful emotion that is our reaction to circumstances, based on our perceptions and beliefs. Anger, like other emotions, is part of being human. However, it is important that students learn how to manage anger so that they can avoid trouble and become productive students. Sometimes the source of anger cannot be removed and coping skills are needed to deal with the anger. Students who have learned applicable coping skills usually fare much better when facing anger-provoking situations.

When students learn coping skills, they gain a set of healthy responses to adverse circumstances that increases their chances to be successful in school. For example, when students learn anger management skills, they will likely improve their behavior in the classroom and school.

The issue of violence and crime so captured the attention of professional educators, parents, and public officials, that safe, disciplined, and drug-free schools that offer an environment conductive to learning is one of the National Education Goals. Since the inception of Goals 2000, schools have made strides in decreasing crime and violence in school, but there is much work yet to do.

Professional educators, parents, and policymakers will likely agree that anger experienced by students has multiple origins. Most will probably agree that many students growing up in poor neighborhoods characterized by rundown housing, poverty, rampant crime, unemployed adults and drug abuse, are prime candidates for committing crime and violence at school. Unfortunately, many of these same students have no choice but to attend schools lacking in sufficient capital and human resources to address their academic and emotional needs. Many schools, even where there are sufficient programs, staff, and curricula, often fall short of addressing the special needs of these students.

Helping students learn how to better deal with anger will reduce the incidence of disruptive incidents in the school. This can result in a more nurturing learning environment that will help students focus more on learning and increase academic achievement.

This section on *Roadblock #2 – Anger*, will provide activities to help students develop coping skills to deal with anger. The activities in this section are designed to stimulate student discussion. Therefore, students may introduce various issues that cannot possibly be included in this material. Professional educators are encouraged to draw from their own experiences and knowledge without imposing their views on the students.

Each activity in this section can be used independently. Each lesson will provide an opportunity for students to get acquainted and/or learn more about each other. In addition, students will develop skills helpful in eliminating anger, which can be a Roadblock to Achievement. You are also invited to select lessons most appropriate for your group. Good Luck and I wish you the best!

GET ACQUAINTED

OBJECTIVE(S):
• To provide opportunities for students to learn more about each other
• To provide an overview of each lesson

PROCEDURE(S):
Have students pair up. Then, have each pair stand facing each other for a minute then turn their backs to one another. While backs are turned have each person change two things about themselves. (for example; put watch or bracelets on opposite wrist, change hair, roll one pant leg up, etc.) See if each person can guess what these changes are.

Display the title of each lesson with brief description of the content of each lesson. Then discuss the reason for each of the lessons.

Discuss the timeline for completing all lessons.

Discuss the goal(s) for the lessons: an opportunity to learn techniques and strategies that could likely improve the quality of their lives.

SUMMARY:
Ask students to share their feelings about what it takes to notice changes in their peers.

30

ACTIVITY 2.1

THE STORMS WITHIN

OBJECTIVE(S):
• To understand the meaning of self-regulation
• Analyze stories of individuals who had problems regulating their own behaviors

PROCEDURE(S):
Display and discuss definition of self-regulation.
Self-regulation: Control own impulses, habit, emotions, feelings, or desires.

Read the following story, *Risky Behavior.*

RISKY BEHAVIOR

Mario, a professional football player, had a bright future ahead of him. In his second year as a professional player, he established new records for the most touchdowns in a single game. They recognized him the first and second year as the most valuable player. Everything looked great for Mario!

Off the field, however, he participated in activities that adversely affected his life. He regularly attended drinking parties, smoked crack cocaine, and drove under the influence of alcohol. He lost his driver's license due to driving under the influence (DUI).

Participation in unhealthy activities in his private life took their toll on his professional football career by his third year in the pros. He frequently showed up late to practice, played halfheartedly in games, and he was often aggressive with his coach and teammates. The owners of the team warned him about his behavior, but the warnings had little effect. Finally, in the middle of the season, they ordered him to sit out for the remainder of the season. They did not renew his contract.

ASK THE FOLLOWING QUESTIONS:
• What changes in Mario's behavior told you something was wrong?
• Did Mario control his behavior? Why or why not?
• How did this affect his life?
• What would have occurred if he had exercised more control?

"THE FIRST AND BEST VICTORY IS TO CONQUER SELF" (PLATO).
Display and discuss this quote. Explain that controlling oneself is often hard to do, but it can be done if you follow and practice certain principles in your life.

DIVIDE STUDENTS INTO GROUPS:
Group students using different colored of marbles, individually wrapped hard or soft candy, pieces of cardstock, or any other items you deem appropriate. Students can draw items from a container while eyes are closed.

THE STORMS WITHIN (CONT.)

Ask students to select a recorder and a spokesperson. The recorder will record the consensus of the group and the spokesperson will report the decisions of the group.

Distribute a copy of the story below to each group. Ask each group of students to read, answer the questions at the end, and report responses to the entire group.

SURPRISE! YOUR MOTHER IS HERE!

Michelle's left her books on her kitchen table. Her mother did not want Michelle to get in trouble for not having her books at school. Her mother brought Michelle's books to the school. When her mother arrived at the school's attendance office, she requested that Michelle be called down to speak with her. The attendance clerk used the intercom system to call into Michelle's classroom and asked her teacher to send Michelle to the attendance office. The teacher responded by stating that Michelle was absent. This shocked her mother. Her mother requested a total number of absences recorded for Michelle from the attendance clerk. The records showed Michelle had been absent for five days out of the fifteen days school was in session. Records also showed that Michelle served three days in-school-suspension (ISS) for cutting classes. When her mother spoke with the vice principal about failure to inform her about Michelle serving detention, the vice principal presented a letter signed by Michelle's mother acknowledging that she was aware of Michelle's absences and her three days in ISS.

Michelle's mother was extremely upset about Michelle cutting school, hiding the letter from the vice principal, and her failure to tell her about serving three days in ISS. Michelle lost most of her privileges and was not able to drive to school for the remainder of the year. She also received one day out of school suspension for forging her mother's signature. When her mother questioned her about her reasons for cutting, she said it was because she was bored and wanted to be with her friends.

QUESTIONS
- What steps could Michelle have taken to avoid cutting school?
- Would it be hard for Michelle to take those steps? Why or why not?
- Do you think cutting school with her friends was worth her losing her mother's trust and her privileges? Why or why not?

Allow each group to make their report. Record group responses on the board and discuss as each is listed. End the lesson by emphasizing the importance of understanding and practicing self-regulating principles (accountability, responsibility, standards). Explain that practicing these principles is necessary to achieving their goal in life. Explain that they will study one principle at a time until all principles are discussed.

ACTIVITY 2.2

THE HUMAN CONNECTION

OBJECTIVE(S):
- To identify the basic needs of human beings.
- Provide an opportunity for students to practice making the connection between behavior and needs.

PROCEDURE(S):
Explain to students that all people have the same basic human needs. It is important to identify, acknowledge, and understand what these basic needs are.

Share with students that William Glasser (2001), a well known psychologist and expert in human behavior, believes that all human beings are constantly trying to satisfy the need to have **fun/laughter** (friends, games, entertainment), **survival** (i.e. food, safety, clothing, shelter), **power/achievement** (i.e. good grades, awards, make own decisions), **belonging** (i.e. group, family, friends, school) and **freedom** (i.e. choices, beliefs, ideas). Discuss these five basic needs with the students and allow them to voice their opinions.

Divide students in small groups of 4 or 5 and distribute worksheet, The Human Connection on following page and the five scenarios to each group. Ask each group to read a scenario and then decide what basic need was not being met. Then, place that particular scenario number under the corresponding need listed on the Human Connection worksheet. Have each group complete all the scenarios. Discuss after they complete the activity.

This reinforces the idea that all human beings have the same basic needs by requiring them to differentiate categories. This practice will enhance their understanding of how each need impacts their behavior and can assist them with developing critical thinking skills, decision making skills, and interpersonal skills.

Discuss responses after students complete the worksheet. Students can also complete this worksheet individually.

This worksheet will provide an opportunity for students to reflect on their own behaviors and the reasons for their behaviors. Students are asked to identify the need they were trying to satisfy when they behaved in a particular manner.

Most students have not been exposed nor have been given opportunities to reflect. For students who have not been given these opportunities, additional guidance on how to self-reflect would be helpful. I often use a personal example to provide a model for students.

Students should leave this lesson with a better understanding of basic human behavior. Behavior may vary based on the individual personality, but the needs are the same. It is important that students also realize that they have the power to determine how they will seek to satisfy these basic human needs. They can choose to satisfy their needs in unhealthy and unproductive ways or satisfy these needs in healthy and productive ways.

THE HUMAN CONNECTION

Directions: Read each of the following scenarios and decide which of the basic needs is not being met. Then, write the scenario number in the appropriate box below. (Then complete page 35)

SCENARIO #1

A student came to school very upset one Monday morning. No one knew why. He hit another student during lunch and was suspended for three days. When the administrator called his mother to pick him up from school, his mother said he left home upset because his father did not pick him up for a game as he promised.

SCENARIO #2

A girl was very smart according to the grades she made in Elementary and Middle schools. Other people thought she was not smart at all. Since she failed her tests and took classes below her ability level. Her friends were in all of her classes.

SCENARIO #3

This student loved to laugh and have fun. But laughter was not allowed in the classroom. But that did not stop him. He laughed in the class and got into trouble many times. He was a likable student, but he just would not stop laughing. He did not laugh at other people, but he laughed at his own jokes and he tried to get others to do the same.

SCENARIO #4

He just gave up. This student tried hard to make good grades, but he just kept making poor grades. He tried hard to ask good questions, but the other students laughed at him when he would ask questions. He tried hard to make the honor roll and never could make it. He tried his best, but then he just gave up.

SCENARIO #5

This had difficult choosing to do the right thing. One night he took his parents car and went to a nightclub that had a bad repetition. His parents did not know he was gone until the policeman brought him home the next morning. It wasn't too long after the nightclub incident that he was in the principal's office for leaving the classroom without permission to go to a nearby restaurant.

SCENARIO #6

This student rarely returns homework and often sleeps in class. She often talks about having to take care of her eleven siblings after school while her mother is at work. Her clothes are usually dirty. Her mother makes minimum wage and gets a paycheck once each month. Part of the mother's paycheck is used for paying a cab to take her to the Laundromat to wash the family's clothes. She qualifies for free lunch but refuses to eat. She is failing her classes.

Survival	Power/ Achievement	Fun/Laughter	Belonging	Freedom

I AM ONLY HUMAN

Directions: Read and respond to each question.

1. What are some examples of unhealthy/unproductive behaviors some people exhibit to acquire what they want?

_____

_____

_____

2. What are some examples of healthy/productive behaviors some people exhibit to acquire what they want?

_____

_____

_____

3. What are some examples of unhealthy/unproductive behaviors you participate in to get what you want?

_____

_____

_____

4. What are some examples of healthy/productive behaviors you participate in to get what you want?

_____

_____

_____

THE WE OF ME
Accountability

OBJECTIVE(S):
- To examine the meaning of accountability.
- Identify individuals to whom they are accountable and in what way they are accountable.
- Help students connect behaviors with accountability.
- Promotes critical thinking and encourages students to analyze their role in avoiding or causing conflict with the people they come in contact with their neighborhood and community

PROCEDURE(S):
Display the definition of accountability.
Accountability: to give a report on; to answer to; to provide an explanation for; to honor.

Divide students into groups. Ask each group to select a recorder and a reporter. Distribute worksheet: **Together We Stand.** Ask students to complete. Discuss group responses.

Distribute worksheet: **The WE of ME** to each group. Ask each group to complete the worksheet. Discuss worksheets after the groups have finished answering the questions. Fifteen minutes should be ample time.

Distribute worksheet: **Give Honor Where Honor Is Due.** Ask each group to select one person or a group of people from each category listed on the board. List behaviors that would honor these individuals and list behaviors that would dishonor them.

Explain that being accountable is to honor people with his/her behavior. When you honor people with your behavior, you are being accountable to them. For example, when you follow your mother's instructions, you are honoring her and therefore being accountable to her. Discuss the groups' responses.

Distribute worksheet: **Someone is Watching You.** Ask students to list at least five people to whom they are accountable on a regular basis. List behaviors they exhibit to demonstrate accountability to these individuals and explain how these behaviors honor these individuals. Allow students to share responses. These activities promote respect and positive regard for other people. It is important that students recognize that human beings are linked together and that we all are accountable to each other. This develops character and enhances the level of sensitivity for each other. This has far reaching educational and social implications. Classrooms and schools will be safe places for students to learn and to enhance their emotional development if most students practice accountability.

SUMMARY:
Close the lesson by challenging each person to honor those they come in contact with today and make a conscious effort to honor people on a continuous basis.

TOGETHER WE STAND

Directions: Think about the people living in your home (i.e. mother, father, grandparent, brother/ sister). Write their names under the column listed "Home." Then think about categories of people living in your neighborhood (i.e. children, elderly people, single adults, parents). List these names under "Neighborhood." Think about ethnic categories of people living in your community (i.e. white, black, Spanish, Indian, Chinese, etc.). List these under "Community." Think about categories of people in your school (students, teachers, administrators, counselors). List them under "School." Now, complete the worksheet, The We of Me.

HOME	NEIGHBORHOOD	COMMUNITY	SCHOOL

THE <u>WE</u> OF ME

Directions: Review the list on the previous worksheet and answer the following questions in the table below for each category

a. How are all these people alike in each category? For example, the people listed under home, how are they alike?

b. How are they different?

c. When you live with or among other people, what behaviors are required of each individual to avoid conflict? For example, how do you avoid conflict with the people in your home, school?

	HOME	NEIGHBORHOOD	COMMUNITY	SCHOOL
ALIKE				
DIFFERENT				
CONFLICT AVOIDING BEHAVIORS				

GIVE HONOR WHERE HONOR IS DUE

Directions: Select one person or a group of people from each category listed on the chart below. List behaviors that would honor these individuals and list behaviors that would dishonor them.

	HOME	NEIGHBORHOOD	COMMUNITY	SCHOOL
PERSON OR GROUP OF PEOPLE				
BEHAVIORS THAT HONOR THIS PERSON OR THIS GROUP OF PEOPLE				
BEHAVIORS THAT DISHONOR THIS PERSON OR THIS GROUP OF PEOPLE				

WORKSHEET

SOMEONE IS WATCHING YOU

Directions: List at least five people to whom you are accountable to on a regular basis. List behaviors you exhibit to demonstrate accountability to these individuals. Explain how these behaviors honor these individuals.

	PERSON #1	PERSON #2	PERSON #3	PERSON #4
NAME OF INDIVIDUAL				
BEHAVIORS THAT DEMONSTRATE ACCOUNTABILITY				
EXPLAIN HOW THESE BEHAVIORS HONOR THIS PERSON				

ACTIVITY 2.4

YOU CAN COUNT ON ME!
Responsibility

OBJECTIVE(S):
- To examine the meaning of responsibility
- To identify responsible behaviors
- To connect behaviors with consequences
- Identify advisors and confidants at home, school, and community

PROCEDURE(S):
Display the definition of responsibility.
Responsibility: The quality or state of being responsible: moral, legal, or mental accountability; reliable, trustworthy; liable to be called upon to answer as the primary cause, motive, or agent.

Divide the students into groups by color of hair, eyes, favorite food, or favorite color.

Distribute: **What Would You Do** worksheet found on the following page. Have students read the scenarios and decide on the action they would take. Write the possible consequences of each action. List the responsible behavior and discuss why you think it is responsible.

Ask students to think of five people they could talk to about anything personal in their lives. Ask them to write the names of these people on a sheet of paper. Explain that these people are those most likely to help them make responsible decisions and hold them accountable for their actions.

SUMMARY:
Summarize by asking students to respond to the following questions:

- Is it important to show others that you are responsible? Why or why not? Discuss.

- What are the benefits of behaving responsibly? Discuss.

- What are some factors and people (i.e. friend, ideas, past experiences, etc.) that could possibly influence your decisions? Discuss.

WHAT WOULD YOU DO?

Directions: Read the scenarios and decide on the action you would take. Write the possible consequences of each action. List the responsible behavior and discuss why you think it is responsible.

SCENARIO 1

You did not study for your math test. You know Samantha is smart and always knows the correct answers. You sit right behind her and can easily copy her answers?

What are two possible actions you can take?

_____

_____

What are the possible consequences of each of your actions?

_____

_____

_____

What would you do?

_____

_____

_____

SCENARIO 2

Your parents forbid you from attending a party where there will be alcohol served. The night of the party, you convince your parents to allow you go to the movies with some friends. You take a detour to the party intending only to stay for thirty minutes. When you check your watch, two hours had passed. You panic and insist that your friends take you home. Your friends have been drinking.

WHAT WOULD YOU DO? (CONT.)

What are two possible actions?

_____

_____

What are the possible consequences of each of your actions?

_____

_____

_____

What would you do?

_____

_____

_____

SCENARIO 3
You saw your best friend steal an item from a department store.

What are two possible actions you can take?

_____

_____

What are the possible consequences of your actions?

_____

_____

_____

What would you do?

_____

_____

_____

ACTIVITY 2.5

THIS IS WHAT I STAND FOR!
Standards

OBJECTIVE(S):
- To examine the meaning of standards
- Connect belief about standards to behavioral choices

PROCEDURE(S):
Display the definition of standards.

Standards: (code of conduct) established by authority, custom, or general consent as a model or example; a means of determining what a thing should be; something set up as a rule for the measure of quantity, weight, extent, value, or quality.

Explain to the students that without established standards, there is no measure by which your behavior or actions can be judged. The standards you choose to observe and practice in your lives will determine the quality of your life. For example, if honesty is chosen as one of your standards, you will likely enjoy the repetition as a person with integrity.

Distribute worksheet: **This Is What I Stand For!** found on the following page. Ask students to read and follow the directions to complete the worksheet. This activity encourages students to think about the standard of behaviors and how these standards influence behavioral choices. Provide personal examples for the students as a model for the activity.

SUMMARY:
Summarize by emphasizing that understanding what students believe about behaviors will help guide their decisions. Standards of behaviors promote peer pressure resilience and develop a confidence as they make decisions based on their standards.

THIS IS WHAT I STAND FOR!

Directions: Respond to the questions below.

1. What do you believe about school? How will this belief likely influence your behavior?

2. What do you believe about rules? How will this belief likely influence your behavior?

3. What do you believe about family? How will this belief likely influence your behavior?

4. What do you believe about friendship? How will this belief likely influence your behavior?

5. What do you believe about being yourself? How will this belief likely influence your behavior?

6. What do you believe about honesty? How will this belief likely influence your behavior?

7. What do you believe about trust? How will this belief likely influence your behavior?

8. What do you believe about fairness? How will this belief likely influence your behavior?

9. What do you believe about integrity? How will this belief likely influence your behavior?

10. What do you believe about race? How will this belief likely influence your behavior?

ACTIVITY 2.6

TURN ABOUT IS FAIR PLAY!

OBJECTIVE(S):
• Provide opportunities for students to examine the cause and effect of behavior

PROCEDURE(S):
Present an apple seed, apple, and any other type of fruit and the seed of that fruit. Ask students to explain what happens when you plant the apple seed. Ask them to explain what happens when you plant the seed of another fruit. Explain to the students that these are examples of cause and effect.

Distribute worksheet: **Turn About Is Fair Play** found on the following page. Ask students to list the cause for each effect on the worksheet.

Ask students to share their responses. Ask students to identify things from the two lists that can be controlled by people. Ask them to identify things from the two lists that cannot be controlled by people. Write their responses on a board, overhead or flip cart.

Explain to students that people can change the outcome by exercising control over the things they can control. For example, you can prevent cavities by brushing, flossing, and decreasing sugar intake. Explain to students that people cannot change the outcome of those things they have no control over.

Explain to students that changing things they can control will change their lives. For example: poor grades, being on restriction, and receiving office referrals.

Have students pair up. Ask one student to raise both hands with palms facing toward their partner. Ask that student to then push against the hands of their partner. Ask them to explain what happened during this activity.

Explain that everything they do has an effect. When they pushed the hands of their partner, the partner pushed back. Explain that in the same way, people's response to them sometimes is a direct result of how they behave and interact with others. Also emphasize to the students that every action has a reaction and every cause has an effect. In order to change the effect, they have to change the cause. Use some examples to further illustrate this point.

SUMMARY:
Summarize by emphasizing the following points:

• You can only change that which you can control.

• To change the effect (outcome), you must change the cause (behavior).

TURN ABOUT IS FAIR PLAY

Directions: List the cause for each effect on the table below.

CAUSE	EFFECTS
	Change from night to day
	War
	Color of eyes
	Skin color
	Depression
	Conflict with others
	Diabetes
	Poor grades
	Cavities
	Getting detention
	Restriction
	Getting arrested
	Being late for school
	Aggression

ACTIVITY 2.7

LET US REASON TOGETHER!
Conflict Resolution

OBJECTIVE(S):
• Provide opportunities for students to examine techniques and strategies for resolving conflicts

PROCEDURE(S):
Ask students to define "Conflict Resolution." Discuss their responses.

Ask students to list behaviors that cause conflict (i.e. name calling, gossiping, revenge, embarrassing, threatening, blaming, taking liberties, failing to take responsibility, bossing, bullying, and sneering).

Explain to the students that people typically deal with conflict in one of three ways. Display the animals describing three ways people typically deal with conflict.

■ OSTRICH - sidesteps the issue. Try to get out of the situation quickly. Try to avoid the issue.

■ LION - refuses to back down. Determined to win.
  -focus on the person rather than the behavior
  -focuses on the problem rather than the solution
  -judges
  -uses insults
  -uses sarcasm
  -threatens
  -blames
  -accuses

■ ANT - deals with the issue. Is willing to listen and find a solution.
This method may include the following techniques:
  -Locating a good place to talk.
  -Locating the most appropriate time to talk.
  -Focusing on the problem.
  -Being an active listener
  -Using clear messages
  -Brainstorming for a solution that works for everyone.

Present the following scenario and allow two students to role play each style (ostrich, lion, and ant) of dealing with conflict. Discuss.

> **SCENARIO: Word has gotten back to Tonya that Lisa, her friend, has been spreading rumors about her being pregnant.**

ACTIVITY 2.7

LET US REASON TOGETHER!
Conflict Resolution
(continued)

Write the components of "active listening" and "clear messages" on a board, flip chart, overhead or display in another manner. Discuss each until you are sure students have a good grasp of the concepts.

ACTIVE LISTENING
- Establish and maintain eye contact.
- Acknowledge what is being said by nodding, saying "uh, huh"
- Check for clarity and understanding by saying back in your own words what the other person said. Do this periodically throughout the conversation.
- Listen for feelings behind the words.

CLEAR MESSAGES
Clear messages do the following:
- Tell the person why you are upset.
- Tell the person how you feel about the matter.
- Tell the person what you need from him or her.
- Tell the person what you do not want or need.
- Seek a solution.

Allow students an opportunity to practice confronting using clear messages.

"When you _____ I feel _____. I need you to _____ the next time instead of _____."

Avoid hostile messages that take a Lion approach:
-Threaten the person.

"I want you to stop _____. If you do not, I'll _____."

Divide students into pairs. Ask students to rotate roles as they use the Ant techniques in the following role-plays:

SCENARIO 1: **You looked everywhere for your necklace. You could not find it. The next day, you recognize what you believe to be your necklace around a young lady's neck.**

SCENARIO 2: **Changing class is hectic. People are shoving and pushing all the time to avoid being late to class. Each day, however, this same student manages to push and shove you against the lockers. You are fed up with his behavior.**

LET US REASON TOGETHER!
Conflict Resolution
(continued)

ACTIVITY 2.7

Ask students to suggest a few scenarios, develop some scenarios, or use the scenarios below to provide role-playing opportunities that emphasize the following points:

- Resolving conflict takes two willing parties.
- Resolving conflict requires talking calmly.
- Resolving conflict requires active listening (showing interest by asking questions, maintaining, eye contact, restating and paraphrasing, and being sensitive to feelings).
- Resolving conflict often requires negotiation.
- Find a suitable place to talk.
- Wait for a good time.
- Remain calm.
- Be respectful of others opinions.
- Resolving conflict requires effective communication; avoid judging, insulting, using sarcasm, threatening, blaming, and accusing.
- Use clear messages.
- Resolving conflict requires an acknowledgment of the problem.
- Agree on what the problem is.

SCENARIOS:

1 You heard that your best friend is seeing your boyfriend.

2 You observe a friend removing an item from the teacher's desk.

3 You see the student who sits next to you in class cheating on a test. You have tried to cover your answers. However, you feel bad about concealing your answers because this is a close friend. You are getting fed up with this behavior, but you also value your friendship with this person.

4 This person constantly picks on you for having a high-pitched voice. Others are also beginning to pick on you because of your voice.

5 Your teacher blames you for everything that goes wrong in the classroom. You admit your behavior is not the best, but it upsets you that your teacher blames you for each incident.

6 You have had some problems in the past with lying. Lately, you have tried to be truthful with everyone. Despite times when there were possible serious consequences, you told the truth. Your parents, however, still do not believe you.

7 You have tried everything you know to please your parents. Nothing seems good enough.

8 Your boyfriend has not been paying much attention to you lately. You suspect he is interested in another girl.

9 This particular customer frequents the fast food restaurant where you work. He always finds something wrong with the food. You do not know how long you can keep from saying something rude to this person. Your company has a policy of "The customer is always right."

10 Your little sister is really upsetting you. Her behavior makes you angry. She cries and complains to your parents about you getting angry. Your parents become upset with you.

LET US REASON TOGETHER!
Conflict Resolution
(continued)

Tell the students that in a conflict there are two individuals, the one who causes the conflict (conflict sender) and the one who is the recipient of the conflict (conflict receiver). In an effort to resolve the conflict, both parties must be willing to compromise. Display the following and discuss.

CONFLICT SENDER
- be willing to acknowledge wrong
- be willing to apologize
- be willing to change behavior
- be willing to evaluate action
- be willing to listen

CONFLICT RECEIVER
- be willing to listen
- be willing to forgive
- be willing to empathize
- be willing to talk
- be willing to state feelings
  about the person's behavior
- be willing to take action if this behavior
  occurs again

SUMMARY:
Summarize by emphasizing the following points to resolve conflicts:
- Be willing to use active listening.
- Be willing to send clear messages.
- Be willing to use effective communication skills.
- Try to see the other person's point of view.
- Be willing to apologize or forgive.

Emphasize that there will always be conflicts in life. Learning how to handle conflicts in a productive way is a skill that can be learned.

ROADBLOCK 3

Student Disconnection

"Not failure, but low aim, is crime."
— James Russell Lowell

INTRODUCTION

Students who feel disconnected from school are likely to have more discipline referrals, involvement in high risk behaviors, and be less involved in school activities than students who feel connected. Schneider and Stevenson (1999) found that for some students who have disconnected, sleep was the most preferred activity.

One reason some students disconnect, according to Mendler (2001), is because they have a lack of confidence in their ability to achieve. The lack of confidence is likely to reduce the student's efforts to complete assigned tasks in the classroom. Often, the lack of effort from the student results in poor grades and low test scores. With each passing year and with each missed opportunity to connect with the learning environment, the student falls behind his or her peers. When students fall behind, some are likely to become targets for ridicule and demeaning comments about their inability to achieve. These comments are likely to come from their peers, but too often such comments are made by some professional educators. These comments could influence how other professional educators interact with these students.

Because it is not "cool" to be smart is another reason many students disconnect from school (Bamburg, 1994). I have counseled with many students over the years that disconnected from school because they wanted to be accepted by their peers. Acceptance by their peers was more important to them than making good grades. Those more concerned about being part of a particular peer group will likely underachieve just to remain "cool."

Another possible explanation of why students disconnect is feeling unappreciated and undervalued at home and at school. When students feel ignored or think they are not valued by others, they tend to disconnect from that environment. William Glasser, theorist and author of *Counseling with Choice Theory* (2001), suggests that the need to belong is a basic human need that most individuals seek to satisfy. If this need to belong is unsatisfied in one situation or group, students will likely seek a group where the need to belong is satisfied.

One place the need to belong could be satisfied is in a school where all students are valued and appreciated. Such a school focuses on the importance of the individual student while providing meaningful lessons and a variety of opportunities for students to achieve. The development of the individual student is the primary concern. When students feel good about themselves, they typically experience an enhanced desire to achieve and the natural result is connecting with school.

Many elementary and middle schools are child-centered while most high schools are organized around subject areas or departments. Students' work is proudly displayed throughout most elementary and middle school buildings. Many high schools tend to display student work from specific departments (i.e. art, and home economics) while student work from other subject areas are many times kept in folders unavailable to others to admire or provide positive feedback. Perhaps high schools could learn a valuable lesson from the elementary and middle schools. The elementary and middle schools seem to understand that when you make the individual more important than the subject, academic achievement is likely to increase.

If some students feel like they do not belong, they will likely underachieve. Schools will increase the possibility of student success by providing caring environments rich with warmth and nourishment capable of connect-

53

ing with the mind and spirit of all students (Lumsden, 1994). Failure to connect with the mind and spirit of students could be another contributing factor to students disconnecting from school. One way of connecting with the minds and spirit of most students is recognizing and celebrating diversity. Recognizing and celebrating diversity enhances the school environment.

Another possible issue related to students disconnecting from school is their concern for fairness and justice. Many students don't feel that they are treated fairly in the school or classroom (Tauber, 1998, Schwartz, 1996, Bamburg, 1994). They feel they are graded more harshly, are referred more for minor offenses, and are not given opportunities to be part of the mainstream student body as are other students. This feeling of exclusion often creates hostile feelings toward teachers, school officials and peers. Exclusionary practices will likely have a negative impact on the entire school program. A system of fairness and equity will increase the probability that all students will believe they are valued and appreciated.

The activities in this section are designed to stimulate discussion. Therefore, students may introduce various issues that cannot possibly be included in this material. Professional educators are encouraged to draw from their own experiences and knowledge without imposing their views on the students. If information is not readily available on issues that students introduce, the professional educator is encouraged to research and inform students of the findings at the next scheduled meeting.

Each activity in this section can be used independently. Each lesson will provide an opportunity for students to get acquainted and/or learn more about each other. In addition, students will understand their interconnectedness with others and how to use these connections as resources to help them reach their full potential. Students will examine beliefs, set goals, explore options, and identify resources in the school and community. Encourage students to see how being disconnected can be a *roadblock to achievement*. You are also invited to select lessons most appropriate for your group. Good Luck and I wish you the best!

GET ACQUAINTED

OBJECTIVE(S):
• To provide opportunities for students to get acquainted
• To provide an overview of the lessons for students

PROCEDURE(S):
Each student will need a large index card or sheet of paper for a nametag. Ask students to follow the directions below:
• Write your name in the center of your card.
• In the upper left corner, write four things that you like to do.
• In the upper right corner, write your four favorite singers or groups.
• In the lower left corner, write your four favorite movies.
• In the lower right corner, write four adjectives, which describe you.

When everyone finishes, ask him or her to do the following:
• Mingle among each other for a few minutes.
• Without talking, read the upper left corner of the card belonging to other students.
• Then, find one or two students who are most like themselves and talk with them for a few minutes.
• Then, mingle among each other reading the upper right corner of the cards belonging to other students.
• Find one or two people most like themselves and talk with them. Repeat with the lower left corner and lower right corner information.

Explain the reason for the lessons and how often the lessons will be held. Explain that they will have an opportunity to learn ways in which they can enhance their lives and to learn techniques that can make their lives more productive.

Provide an overview of each lesson by displaying the title of each lesson with brief statements of the content.

SUMMARY:
Ask students to share their feelings about participating in the get acquainted lesson.

ACTIVITY 3.1 — YOU ARE WHAT YOU THINK!

OBJECTIVE(S):
- To examine the belief system of students and how their belief system developed
- To examine the relationship between their beliefs and their behavior

PROCEDURE(S):
"Change your beliefs and you change your life" (Norman Vincent Peale). Display and discuss.

Distribute worksheet: **Fact or Illusion?** Ask students to follow directions and complete.

Note: Emphasize that beliefs can influence how we react or behave. Just like some of these animals have a bad reputation, we can too. Rumors are not always factual.

Explain to the students that beliefs are formed by observing and interacting with significant others (provide examples of significant others) and with the environment (TV, ads, movies, etc.). As these beliefs become an established part of your subconscious and consciousness, your behavior will likely reflect these beliefs.

Explain to the students that an examination of the origins of their beliefs and how their beliefs affect their behavior will provide opportunities to decide if their beliefs are faulty and need reworking. Read the following examples of "faulty" beliefs.

EXAMPLES OF FAULTY BELIEFS
- There is only one way to do things.
- My way is the only way.
- The more money you have, the happier you are.
- If everyone does not like me, I am not OK.
- Blonds have more fun.
- You need alcohol to enjoy life.
- The more friends I have, the happier I will be.
- Everyone is doing it.

*Faulty Beliefs - Any belief that hinders productivity and causes problems in your life.

Explain to students that beliefs will vary from person to person on the same issues. For example, some people believe people as a whole can be trusted. Others believe no one can be trusted and you need to be suspicious of everyone.

YOU ARE WHAT YOU THINK! (CONT.)

Discuss: If you trust others, how will your behavior reflect this belief? If you don't trust others, how will your behavior reflect this belief?

Read several behavioral scenarios (taken from newspaper clippings or magazine articles) to the students. Ask them to identify the person's belief(s) by evaluating the behavior of the individual. Discuss.

Provide students with some examples of beliefs (i.e. all snakes are dangerous, all people lie, teachers are mean, parents are old fashioned, most teens drink alcohol). Ask students to discuss probable behaviors of individuals possessing such beliefs.

Provide some teen magazines or magazines which contain advertisements directed toward teens. Ask, "What kind of faulty beliefs do the advertisements display?"

Ask students to write down their faulty beliefs that cause them problems and a new belief that could replace the faulty one.

SUMMARY:
Summarize by emphasizing the following points:
• Beliefs affect behavior.
• Beliefs can change.
• Significant others in our environment help shape our beliefs.
• Environmental influences help shape our beliefs.

FACT OR ILLUSION?

Directions: Read and answer the questions about each animal on this worksheet.

1. **How would you describe each of these animals?**
2. **Where did you get your information? Is there only one answer?**
3. **What do you believe is true about each animal?**
4. **If you came in contact with any of these animals, what would you do? Why?**

PIT BULL

1. _____
2. _____
3. _____
4. _____

SNAKE

1. _____
2. _____
3. _____
4. _____

ALLIGATOR

1. _____
2. _____
3. _____
4. _____

SKUNK

1. _____
2. _____
3. _____
4. _____

TIGER

1. _____
2. _____
3. _____
4. _____

DOG

1. _____
2. _____
3. _____
4. _____

WHEN IN ROME

ACTIVITY 3.2

OBJECTIVE(S):
• Examine various cultures as they relate to relationships and environments.

PROCEDURE(S):
Define and discuss the meaning of culture.

Identify the characteristics of a culture.
Note: If they do not mention the following attributes, you should include them:

- language
- styles of clothing
- styles of hair
- customs
- food
- laws
- moral expectations
- religion

Explain to students that this lesson will focus on the various cultures as they relate to relationships and environments. List the following on the board, overhead, flip chart or display in another manner. Ask students to fill in the characteristics that are present in a school culture.

Style of clothing...............	Language...................
Style of hair......................	Customs....................
Food..................................	Rules.........................
Peer Groups.....................	Music........................

Continue with the same procedure for teen culture, neighborhood culture, street culture, home culture, black culture, white culture, and gang culture.

Discuss the differences among the various cultures - compare and contrast them.

Ask the students the following questions:
- Is it important to recognize and to know the characteristics of the various cultures? Why or why not?
- How can this information help you?
- Is it important at times to ignore cultural expectations? When? Why?

SUMMARY:
Summarize by emphasizing the following points:
- Different cultural situations demand different responses and behaviors.
- Deviations from cultural expectations should be considered when they will cause harm to self and others. It is important to remember that "you are limited only by the appropriateness and lawfulness of the activity."

ACTIVITY 3.3

THE BALL IS IN YOUR COURT

OBJECTIVE(S):
- To formulate a meaning of goal attainment
- To specify the components of goal attainment

PROCEDURE(S):
Explain to students that setting goals is an important habit to form and incorporate into their lives. However, too often the focus on goal setting is on goal attainment. Once the goal is set – then what? Success does not come by merely setting goals, but by reaching those goals. For that reason, the focus of this lesson is goal attainment.

Distribute worksheet with the four keys to goal attainment and discuss when students complete them.

KEY #1: Preparation   KEY #2: Attitude   KEY #3: Tenacity   KEY #4: Caring

Distribute worksheet: **The Ball Is In Your Court.** Ask students to complete the worksheet. Ask students to share their responses.

SUMMARY:
Summarize by emphasizing the following points:
- Preparation, attitude, tenacity, and caring are the four most important keys to success.
- Goal attainment is the only way to realize your dreams.
- Always be willing to start over again! If you fail, try, try, and try again!

KEY 1: PREPARATION

PREPARATION is defined in the Webster dictionary as "the action or process of making something ready for use or service or of getting ready for some occasion, test, or duty." Preparation plays a big part in success and being appropriately prepared for any task. Preparation is a key to attaining one's goals.

Directions: Answer the questions below and share your answers with others. Describe how you would prepare for each of the following:

1. Final Exam

_____

_____

2. SAT or ACT

_____

_____

3. Driver's License

_____

_____

4. A Career

_____

_____

What would happen if you were not prepared for each one?

KEY 2: ATTITUDE

ATTITUDE is defined in the Webster dictionary as a "feeling or emotion towards a fact or state." An "I can" and an "I will" attitude will increase your chance of success. Both "I can" and "I will" attitudes are necessary. You must believe you can perform (I can) and are willing (I will) to perform. Remember: *"Whether you think you can or think you can't … you are right!"*

Directions: Read and respond to the following questions.

Elaine

Elaine woke up in the hospital with her loved ones at her bedside. She opened her mouth but was unable to speak. Her friend reached for a paper and pencil. Elaine had some difficulty holding the pencil, but she managed to write "What happened?" Since her hearing was not affected, her friend responded, you had a stroke. Shocked, Elaine's eyes teared up and she cried for hours. That was the last time she cried about having a stroke. Since that day, Elaine always smiled and responded positively when asked, "How are you doing?" Her favorite response was, "I am doing great." Elaine was in rehabilitation for one year. She worked hard and had to endure some painful challenges and she fought her way back to health.

1. **What kind of attitude did Elaine have about her illness?**

2. **Do you think this attitude helped her work to get well?**

3. **What would have happened if she had the opposite attitude?**

4. **What can you learn from Elaine's story that can help you?**

5. **What do you think is the main reason for Elaine's attitude?**

KEY 3: TENACITY

TENACITY is defined in the Webster dictionary as "persistence." Tenacity is a key to being successful.

Display and discuss:

"To achieve — keep your heart on your work, your mind on your task, your eyes on your goal, and go!"

— *Harry C. Mabey*

Directions: Read the questions below and respond. Share you responses with others.

1. What was one of the hardest tasks you ever had to complete?

2. What steps did you take to complete the task?

3. What did you learn from completing that task that will help you to complete other difficult tasks in the future?

4. How can you use what you learned from completing this task to help others?

KEY 4: CARING

CARING means putting your heart into whatever you choose to do. Caring includes traits such as honesty, integrity, and compassion.

Directions: Read and respond to the following questions. Share your responses with others.

1. **When was the last time someone showed they cared about you?**

2. **What did they do to show you that they cared?**

3. **When was the last time you cared about someone?**

4. **How did they know you cared about them?**

5. **When was the last time you cared about a project or task?**

6. **What did you do to show you care about the task or project?**

7. **How can caring help you reach your goals?**

THE BALL IS IN YOUR COURT

It is essential for you to set goals and to reach those goals. It is important for you to know that long-term goals require time. Long-term goals are generally accomplished one step at a time. Each step will require specific action from you. Some people call these steps, short-term goals.

Once you have decided on your long-term goals, you will want to plan your short-term goals (steps) to help you reach your long-term goals. Below, write two goals you want to accomplish within the next year. Then write your short-term goals (steps) to help you reach your long-term goal. Indicate the date you plan to start working on your short-term goals. These goals could include career goals, personal goals, academic goals, family goals, etc.

YOU MUST TAKE ACTION TO REACH YOUR GOALS

LONG TERM GOALS	SHORT TERM GOALS
	Step 1: Step 2: Step 3: Step 4: Step 5: Start Date:
	Step 1: Step 2: Step 3: Step 4: Step 5: Start Date:

ACTIVITY 3.4

DESIRES OF THE HEART!

OBJECTIVE(S):

• To explore career choices

PROCEDURE(S):

Invite a career counselor to talk to the students about careers and to administer a simple career inventory. Some simple career inventories are self-scoring and can be discussed during the same class meeting. If you do not have a career counselor, the school counselor will be able to assist you with this lesson.

Discuss different careers and the requirements for each.

Ask students to select their top three-career choice (prioritize their choices) and write the requirements for each career choice. Students can use resources from the media center or resources provided by the school or career counselor. Then, have students take turns sharing their top career choices.

SUMMARY:

Summarize by having students share what they discovered they had in common with the career choices of their peers, family members, and other adult role models.

ACTIVITY 3.5

IT IS WRITTEN

OBJECTIVE(S):
• To provide information to students about laws governing juvenile delinquent behavior

PROCEDURE(S):
Invite the school resource officer or an officer from the juvenile division of the local police department to talk with students about the laws regarding juvenile offenders.
Ask the officers if they can use real case examples.

Discuss how many juvenile offenders have had negative experiences with school and academics. Ask students to brainstorm ways to help these students before they get into trouble.

Discuss what truancy is and ask students to brainstorm ideas for reducing truancy.

Discuss discipline problems students exhibit in school. Ask students to brainstorm ideas for reducing referrals for discipline.

SUMMARY:
Provide an opportunity for students to ask questions of the officer.

ACTIVITY 3.6 — FOR A GOOD CAUSE

OBJECTIVE(S):
• To familiarize students with agencies which provide opportunities to volunteer

PROCEDURE(S):
Invite community agencies to participate as part of a panel. Panelists can share how and where one may volunteer in their agencies.

Suggested panelists:
• Parks and Recreation
• Representative from community centers
• Local hospital
• Churches
• School official
• Local businesses
• Local Police Department (The Explorers)
• School Resource Officer

Take the information from the career inventory you completed in activity #4. Using that information, about your #1 choice, name 4 volunteer opportunities that would help you learn more about that particular career.

SUMMARY:
Allow students to ask questions and allow panelists to emphasize important points.

ACTIVITY 3.7 NOBLE INTENTIONS

OBJECTIVE(S):
- To familiarize students with job opportunities available in their community
- To provide information about the application process and Do's and Don'ts of an interview

PROCEDURE(S):
Invite individuals from various companies to speak with students about job opportunities or ask the career counselor to speak with your students.

Suggested Companies:
- Job Service
- Local Fast Food Restaurants
- Community agencies
- Local Grocery Stores
- Chamber of Commerce
- Local Business Owners

Ask the career counselor to work with each student to help them find employment or solicit the help of a job coach.

If time permits have students role play mock interviews.

SUMMARY:
Summarize by allowing students to ask questions of company representatives.

STRUCTURING GROUPS

This section is to be used by counselors or other professional educators for small groups outside the classroom.

SELECTING STUDENTS

1. Teachers will be asked to select students who exhibit three or more characteristics in each of the three categories of concerns listed on the following page.

2. Teachers will be asked to complete a referral form. Part A is to be completed before the initial meeting.

3. Teachers will be asked to complete part A of the referral form on each child referred for group counseling.

4. A maximum of seven students is recommended for a small group. It may be necessary to form several groups to accommodate all referrals. Small groups are usually held in six to eight week cycles.

5. At the end of the cycle, teachers will be asked to complete part B of the referral form for each student. This will help to evaluate the success of the activities and will provide feedback for improvement in future groups.

6. Students are asked to complete an evaluation form at the end of each cycle. Results will be tallied, analyzed, and share with appropriate school personnel.

SCHEDULING STUDENTS

Students will meet once each week on a rotating basis according to their schedules. Teachers and administrators will be provided a timeline outlining dates, times and places.

NUMBER OF STUDENTS

A small group is recommended due to the nature of the program and activities. I recommend no more than seven students in a group.

WHO CAN PARTICIPATE

All students are invited to participate by referral only.

TIME LINE

There are three sections with seven or eight activities in each section. The timeline will depend upon the section the counselor is using with a particular group.

Evaluation

Discipline records will be secured from previous years or from the current year up to the time of referral. If records are not available, teachers and administrators may be able to provide other discipline information.

Grades for the previous year will be secured or current grades up to the time of referral will be secured from each teacher or from a computerized student information system.

Attendance records will be secured from previous year and compared with attendance after completion of group.

Success of activities will be evaluated on the basis of the following criteria:

- Reduction in number of discipline referrals to an administrator or behavioral specialist.

- Improvement in overall GPA from the previous year.

- Decrease in the number of times inappropriate classroom behavior is addressed by teachers.

- Better attendance.

CATEGORIES OF CONCERN

Name of Student _____ Grade _____

Teacher _____ Date _____

Please check the items that describe this student.

CATEGORY #1: ACADEMIC
Loss of interest in school as evidenced by:

- ❑ Poor grades
- ❑ Failure to complete and turn in homework
- ❑ Failure to complete most classroom assignments
- ❑ Inattentiveness in class
- ❑ Failure to bring books and other materials to class
- ❑ Frequent absences

CATEGORY #2: BEHAVIOR
Lack of self-control and self-discipline as evidenced by:

- ❑ Disrespect and hostile toward authority figures
- ❑ Lying
- ❑ Failure to comply with rules
- ❑ Involved in high risk behaviors (smoking, alcohol, drugs, sex, bullying, threatening other students, etc.)
- ❑ Refuses challenging tasks
- ❑ Complains of being treated unfairly by others in most situations
- ❑ Fails to accept responsibility for own actions
- ❑ Argumentative
- ❑ Disrespectful and hostile towards other students
- ❑ Steals or cheats

CATEGORY #3: MOTIVATION
Lack of concrete goals as evidenced by:

- ❑ Inability to articulate goals
- ❑ Cannot specify steps to achieve goals
- ❑ Lacks thorough knowledge of personal strengths
- ❑ Over emphasizes weaknesses
- ❑ Unable to write down specific goals
- ❑ Gives up easily

REFERRAL/EVALUATION Form

Please complete <u>Part A ONLY</u> and Categories of Concern.

Please return to _____.

PART A

Name of student _____

Present Grade _____ Name of referring teacher_____

Date of birth _____ Age _____

Parent/Guardian _____

Address _____

Race _____ Sex _____

Home Phone _____ Current Grade _____

Number of discipline referrals to date in your class_____

Please list most common reasons for discipline referrals. _____

_____

Dates of Referrals _____

Current academic performance _____

Please mark the items on the attached sheet, Categories of Concern, which describes this student's academic performance, behavior, and motivation.

PART B

To be completed after the student has completed the lessons in a cycle.

1. Name of student _____

2. Number of referrals _____ since _____ (Date lessons began)

3. Please describe the student's present academic performance in your class.

4. Please describe the student's present behavior in your class.

5. Do you feel this group has had a positive effect on the student? ❑ YES ❑ NO
   Explain.

6. Would you recommend this group to others?

STUDENT EVALUATION Form

Please respond to the questions below.

Name _____ (optional)   Date _____

- **What did you learn about yourself as a result of participating in this group?**
  _____
  _____

- **How can you use what you learned to help improve your life?**
  _____
  _____

- **What did you like most about the group?**
  _____
  _____

- **Which activity did you like most?**
  _____
  _____

- **Which activity did you like the least?**
  _____
  _____

- **What suggestions for improvement would you like to offer?**
  _____
  _____

- **Would you recommend this group to other students?** ❑ YES   ❑ NO

- **Would you like to participate in another group that could help you learn skills to improve your life?** ❑ YES   ❑ NO

APPENDIX

AUXILIARY ACTIVITIES

These activities can be completed at the convenience of the student.

1. Visit the school or public library and research the meaning of his or her name. Bring findings back to the class or group.

2. Visit the school or public library and research the events that occurred on the same day, month, and/or year he or she was born. The student can also use the newspaper or other date books. (If students do not know the day they were born, the teacher may want to provide them with a perpetual calendar)

3. Visit the school or public library and research individuals who have made contributions to our society who were born in the same year, month, or day.

4. Visit the school or public library and research famous individuals who have made contributions to our society.

EMPOWERMENT CEREMONY

SUCCESS STARTS WHEN A PERSON FEELS EMPOWERED OR AUTHORIZED TO BE... TO DO...TO BECOME...

This statement clearly attests to the idea of how ones view of oneself will likely affect achieving goals and personal excellence. A feeling of empowerment encourages students to seek the means necessary to attain desired outcomes.

Ceremonies and celebrations (weddings, birthdays, graduations, bar mitzvahs, etc.) are often used to signify a new start and outlook on life. Celebrations/ceremonies provide a sense of empowerment to the person involved in the event.

It is my hope that a ceremony will give the same sense of empowerment to the participants of this program. If the students believe they can improve themselves, they will more likely seek to behave in appropriate and acceptable ways.

Affirmation activities will take on a greater meaning if the student feels empowered or authorized to behave in a positive manner.

Whatever format used, celebration should be the theme and activities should be chosen based on the probability that they will move the student to action. Ceremonies should leave an indelible mark on participants in this program.

Participating in a motivational ceremony could provide a sense of empowerment and thereby encourage the students to continue with renewed optimism. Additionally, it could be the culminating event to provide closure for all previous activities.

SUGGESTIONS:

1. Have students take turns reading one of the following "Affirmations" to provide closure to the program.

2. Invite a motivational speaker to come to your school.

3. Have one of the students prepare a motivational speech to the entire student body.

4. Provide refreshments and invite parents.

5. Award certificates for completion.

6. Have students read the following pledge.

AFFIRMATIONS

I am THE FUTURE. *I am* A DREAMER. *I am* A CREATOR.

I am THE PROMISE OF TOMORROW. *I am* WISE. *I am* A GOOD DECISION MAKER.

I am A RESPONSIBLE PERSON *I am* FILLED WITH TALENTS AND GIFTS.

I am SUCCESSFUL. *I am* A GOOD STUDENT. *I am* A GOOD PERSON.

I am LOVABLE. *I am* A KIND PERSON. *I am* THE BEST ME THAT I CAN BE.

I am SMART IN MANY AREAS. *I am* MY MOTHER'S CHILD. *I am* MY DADDY'S CHILD.

I am A THINKER. *I am* A BELIEVER and BELIEVE IN MANY THINGS. *I am* A PLANNER.

A PLEDGE TO ME

"My name is important and I will treat it with respect by always writing it neat, legibly and with pride.

I know that language, customs, religion, style, music, art, holidays, rituals, tradition, family, life, dress, flag, hairstyle, and diet make up culture. I also acknowledge that there are many different cultures. Nevertheless, no matter where I am or what culture I choose to embrace, I will do so with dignity. I will try to add something of value to my culture from which others can benefit.

I entered this world on _____. Others were born on this day that has made tremendous contributions to society. I will seek also to make a worthwhile contribution to society by using my skills I find through education and my gift given me.

I know goals will help me give ORDER ALONG LIFE'S PATH. Therefore, I will set goals as necessary and make adjustments as needed to meet these goals, I must be prepared, have an "I CAN" and "I WILL" attitude, use all available resources to improve and gain additional knowledge, and exhibit responsibility and courage.

I will strive to be the best person in my family I can be. I will share love, kindness, respect, concern, support, and model acceptance of every member.

I know that it is up to me to allow others to discourage me through peer pressure, difficult situations, conflict with others, racism, prejudice, drugs, stealing, and lying. Nevertheless, I know if I have a positive attitude, work hard, am determined, respect myself and others, practice self-government, set goals, exhibit responsibility, and have trust in a higher authority, these things cannot destroy me.

Like all of creation, I know I have a special purpose for being here on earth. I will daily seek to discover my purpose for that day. It is my hope that whatever my unique purpose is for each given day, I will fulfill it with enthusiasm and gratitude for being chosen for that task-whatever it may be, from getting someone a drink to completing my home work assignments.

I know I must respect myself before others will respect me. What I do and say will tell others how I see myself. Therefore, from this day on, I will hold and carry myself in a way that will show others that I do have self-respect.

As a human being, I know I have the power to choose. I will strive to make proper and responsible choices in all areas of my life; school, home, and community. I also know that part of being a responsible person is being willing to accept all consequences that are rightly due me because of poor decisions.

I know I play many roles; brother, sister, friend, student, son, daughter, etc. Each role brings responsibility. I will therefore fulfill each role to the best of my ability so that I will be a positive influence on others.

REFERENCES

Coil, C. (1999). *Motivating underachievers: 220 Strategies for success.* Revised and Expanded Edition. Marion: IL. Pieces of Learning.

Glasser, W. (2001). Counseling with choice theory: The new reality therapy.

McFadden, A. and Cooper, K. (2004). *Leave no angry child behind: The ABC's of anger management for grades k-12.* Chapin: SC. YouthLight, Inc.

Payne, R. (2003). *A framework for understanding poverty.* (Third rev. ed.). Highlands: TX. Aha! Process, Inc.

Anderman, Lynley Hicks-Midgley, Carol. 1998-06-00 Motivation and Middle School Students http://www.ed.gov/databases/ERIC_Digests/ed421281.html

Author Unknown. 1990-00-00 Positive Discipline http://www.ed.gov/databases/ERIC_Digests/ed327271.html

Author Unknown 1990-00-00 Managing Inappropriate Behavior in the Classroom http://www.ed.gov/databases/ERIC_Digests/ed371506.html

Barbara Gross Davis 1999-9-00 Motivating Students University of California http://www.hcc.hawaii.edu/intranet/committees/FacDevCom/guidebk/teachtip/motiv.hmtl.

Bonwell, Charles C.-Eison, James A. 1991-09-00 Active Learning: Creating Excitement in the Classroom http://www.ed.gov/databases/ERIC_Digests/ed340272.html

Brooks, Vicki; Coll, Ken. 1994 "Troubled Youth: Identification and Intervention Strategies." ERIC Digest" ERIC Clearinghouse on Higher Education Washington, DC. ED371274

Churukian, George A. 1982 "Perceived Learning in the Classroom and Teacher-Student Interpersonal Relationships." ERIC Digest" ERIC Clearinghouse on Higher Education Washington, DC. ED218273

Claxton, Charles S.- Murrell, Patricia H. 1988-00-00 "Learning Styles . ERIC Digest" ERIC Clearinghouse on Higher Education Washington, DC. ED301143 http://www.ed.gov/Databases/ERIC_Digests/ed301143.html

Coballes-Vega, Carmen. 1992-01-00 "Considerations in Teaching Culturally Diverse Children ERIC Digest" ERIC Clearinghouse on Teacher Education Washington, D.C. ED341648 http://www.ed.gov/databases/ERIC_Digests/ed341648.html

Donnelly, Maragarita. 1987-00-00 "At Risk Students". ED292172 ERIC Clearinghouse on Educational Management. Eugene, OR. http://www.ed.gov/databases/ERIC_Digests/ed292172.html

Griggs, Shirley- Dunn, Rita. 1996-05-00 "Hispanic-American Students and Learning Style. ERIC Digest", Eric Clearinghouse on Elementary and Early Childhood Education. Urbana, IL., ED393607, http://www.ed.gov/databases/ERIC_Digests/ed393607.html

❯ REFERENCES *(continued)*

Gaustad, Joan. 1992-12-00 "School Discipline"
http://www.ed.gov/databases/ERIC_Digests/ed350727.html

Gushee, Matt. 1984-00-00 "Student Discipline Policies." ERIC Clearinghouses on Educational Management: ERIC Digest, Number 12. ERIC Clearinghouse on Educational Management. Eugene, OR. ED259455 http://www.ed.gov/database/ERIC_Digests/ed259455.hmtl.

Hitz, Randy-Driscoll, Amy. 1989-00-00 "Praise in the Classroom"
http://www.ed.gov/databases/ERIC_Digests/ed313108.html

Holbrook, Hilary Taylor. 1987-00-00 "Communication Apprehension: The Quiet Student in Your Classroom"
http://www.ed.gov/databases/ERIC_Digests/ed284315.html

Irshmer, Karen. 1996-01-00 "Communication Skills"
http://www.ed.gov/databases/ERIC_Digests/ed390114.html

Jewett, Jan. 1992-00-00 "Aggression and Cooperation: Helping Young Children Develop Constructive Strategies" http://www.ed.gov/databases/ERIC_Digests/ed351147.html

June 1992 "Hard Work and High Expectations: Motivating Students to Learn"
http://www.kidsource.com/kidsource/content3/work.expectation.k12.4.html

Kohn, Alfie. 1994-12-00 "The Risks of Rewards"
http://www.ed.gov/databases/ERIC_Digests/ed376990.html

Lambeth, Charlotte Reed. 1981 "Teacher Invitations and Effectiveness"
http://www.ed.gov/databases/ERIC_Digests/ed201678.html

Lee, Courtland C. 1991-12-31 "Empowering Young Black Males"
http://www.ed.gov/databases/ERIC_Digests/ed341887

Lumsden, Linda. 1997-07-00 "Expectations for Students"
http://www.ed.gov/databases/ERIC_Digests/ed409609

Lunde, Povlacs Joyce. "101 Things You Can Do the First Three Weeks of Class"
http://www.unl.edu/teaching/101ways.html

Marion, Marian. 1997-12-00 "Helping Young Children Deal with Anger"
http://www.ed.gov/databases/ERIC_Digests/ed414077.html

Pallas, Aaron M. 1989-00-00 "Making Schools More Responsive to At-Risk Students"
http://www.ed.gov/databases/ERIC_Digests/ed316617

Sanchez, William – and Others. 1995-00-00 "Working with Diverse Learners and School Staff in a Multicultural Society." Digest" ERIC Clearinghouse on Counseling and Student Services. Greensboro, N.C, American Psychological Association, Washington, D.C. ED390018 http://www.ed.gov/databases/ERIC_Digests/ed390018.html

REFERENCES *(continued)*

Schwartz, Wendy. 2001-12-00 "Closing Achievement Gap: Principles for Improving the Educational Success of All Students"
http://www.ed.gov/databases/ERIC_Digests/ed460191.html

Schwartz, Wendy. 2001-09-00 "School Practices for Equitable Discipline of African American Students"
http://www.ed.gov/databases/ERIC_Digests/ed455343.html

Smith, Francie. 1990 "From Dysfunctional Families to Dysfunctional Schools: A Systems Paradigm."
http://www.ed.gov/databases/ERIC_Digests/ed327785.html

Warger, Cynthia-Burnette, Jane. 2000-08-00 "Five Strategies To Reduce Overrepresentation of Culturally and Linguistically Diverse Students in Special Education"
http://www.ed.gov/databases/ERIC_Digests/ed447627.html